SAI BHASKAR REDDY NAKKA

Amazing Life in Villages and Sustainability

Contents

Introduction

The villages were the dots where the civilisations emerged and flourished. Over many years, some villages have grown into megacities too. The harmony and integrity existed in the villages is becoming rare. The communications and globalisation have penetrated the intricate fabric of villages. Communities living in the villages are no more isolated. Villagers are leaving the old houses and moving away from the water sources to the ridge areas where main roads are existing.

The villages are becoming less sustainable. The village economies contribution to the GDP of the nations is minimal. Many communities have become dependent on the governments. Although the primary sector is essential for sustenance of life, for governments, they are less valuable concerning revenue generation. Many villages are like museum pieces, to sustain their existence governments are implementing many schemes. Without such interventions, many villages would be abandoned or become lost villages, and there would be a mass exodus of the population to the urban areas.

In this book, the glimpses of the village life is presented. The author is having a broad understanding about the villages, having travelled extensively and visited more than ten thousand villages in parts of India and other developing countries.

Memories of a small village

I have so many memories from the time spent in the villages since childhood. Regadi Mamidipally is one such village; it is the native place of my mother located about 75 km from Hyderabad. In the 1970s and 1980s, there were very few transportation means. To reach the village, we used to walk about 10 km all the way from Koukuntla gate, via Chanugomla village crossing Sangamla Vagu. During the rainy season, as this village had black cotton soils predominantly, it was almost impossible to walk with chappals as the soil will hold the feet and slippers. Especially after reaching the village, it was even more difficult. The thorns of "Nalla Thumma" or Acacia nilotica used as fencing to protect the fields from domestic animals, pierced the wet foot without any mercy. Some thorns were mixed with the black damp mud, it was challenging to identify. Finally after reaching the village, would be directed to Jarat (an open place for washing and bathing in the center of the house.) for washing the feet.

In those days, how one could guess that they reached a village habitation? At first, one would smell the Farm Yard Manure or compost from the Pentalu (farmyard manure compost pits) on either side of the road leading to the habitation. Some people had Doddis close to the habitations. Doddi is a place with few trees and with vegetative boundary. The domestic animals were kept, along with the dry grass which was used as fodder and the compost pits. Sometimes the family members also used the Doddi place as an open toilet in turns.

I was born there in the same house where my mother was born, assisted by a Mantrasani (midwife). The tradition was that daughters delivered their babies at the mother's place.

The Soppa (stalks of Sorghum) were kept in the fields as heaps after harvesting. Soppa is used as fodder, its outer bark is thin and razor sharp, and sometimes one might get cuts. I loved to jump from the soppa heaps. It was very dangerous. My Mama warned me not to jump. The white colour soft pith and the sharp bark of the stalks were used for making artefacts. We made beautiful toys such as bullock carts, pull carts and ornaments with it.

In the Pedda Vagu (a big stream, which is also called Esi River) very close to the village, my Mama had a Mota Bhavi, which is an open well adjoining the stream. It is recharged continuously by the subsurface flow of water beneath the sand. From this well, the water was drawn for irrigation using a large-sized iron bucket tied to a rope and usually pulled by a pair of bullocks. A Girka (a wooden pulley wheel) was used attached to a pair of granite posts handing over the open well. The bucket bottom was made up of a leather tube, while pulling up the bucket it was closed with a string, for letting the water flow, the string was released. I used to sit on the frame connected to the large iron bucket and the bullocks and go to and fro while my Mama irrigated the fields.

Annually the Farm Yard Manure was taken from the compost pits and spread in the fields in the peak summer, that is before the arrival of monsoon rains. Often the manure was dug using a Dante (a wooden scrapper) and collected in the vine baskets and was lifted onto the Bullock carts and spread in the fields. The compost appears in the colour of coffee or dark chocolate. The mature compost always smells very good. This compost collected from the pits was accumulated over a period of 10 months.

Often I visited the village during the summer holidays. Jonna Ambali (sorghum gruel) was the favourite drink to beat the heat. It was taken by munching the fresh mango pickle or raw onions. 'Pachhi pulusu' is a soup used for eating with rice or rotis, and sometimes we drank it too. It is an easy dish; it was made up of mainly the liquid extracted from tamarind pods. The pods are soaked in water and squeezed. Some freshly cut onions and green-chilly pieces are added in it along with some salt. This gave a lot of coolness to the body from the summer heat. Shega (the burnt sensation while passing urine) was very common when we spent time in the summer heat. To beat shega we also drank lots of water.

Mulkatte that is a stick with a steel needle at one end, it was used to ward off stray animals eating the crops or to make the bullocks tied to a cart move forward by gently piercing their hips. One could see the blood oozed as points and dried on either side of the bullocks hips. Some people use Charnakola (or a whip) to control the animals. The whip was made with a combination of leather and jute material.

The onions were ready for harvesting in the summers. For storing the onions, the Ulligadda Mande was constructed. Mande is an elongated structure, prepared with the stone pillars and the walls are covered with Kandi Katte or pigeon pea sticks. The top was covered with grass. The porous shelter with aeration increased the storability of the onions. The women by sitting under the shade of tamarind trees cleaned them of the straw and stored in them.

Villagers are afraid when they see Kodangalu (black faced Langoors) in the village. Kodangalu damage the crop and also break the roof tiles. The monkeys (Rhesus macaques) in the villages also cause lots of damage.

In those days electricity supply to the villages was not regular. To pump water from open wells and the stream bed, some people used diesel pump sets. To start them cattle dung water is poured into the pipes first. And by rotating the handle, the engine is started. They made lots of noise and heard up to a kilometre or more distance.

Chelma (water oozing from depression in the stream bed) is the source of drinking water when one is in the open. This water was always cool and fresh. People rarely used pesticides and chemical fertilizers, so the water was clean. Cattle also drank from those chelmas. As the water always flows out of a chelma it is never contaminated. People also drank like animals with their mouth directly touching the surface of water and bending knees and two hands.

At my mother's village, my uncle had two big bullocks bought from Belgaum. They were called Ram-aha and Bheem-aha. These animals were next to the house for extra care. Once I was standing at the main door and they have just arrived. One of them hit me with its horns. I fell down, and there was a fracture to my hand. It took several days, we went to Shalibanda for a bandage, and later my mother using Saraswathi Leaves heated on a pan with a pinch of oil tied every night.

Bullock cart was very interesting for me. I travelled many times in the villages, I have visited. After my brother-in-law's marriage, we all travelled on a chain of bullock carts to their wife's place. It was so beautiful and always cherished this journey. Once my sister was playing on the road, and there was a bullock cart which came running very fast, and it went over her, but nothing happened to her as a miracle. In the villages, we find many people who have broken their bones while travelling on the rough roads of the villages and especially while crossing Vodkalu (small streams). My dream was to have a bullock cart procession with family members at the time of my marriage. I did not happen as I got married in the city, so on my marriage invitation card, the bullock cart picture was there.

In the evening sitting on the Arugu (a platform along the wall of the house) was the favourite place. It facilitated many visitors and friends to come and sit for discussions and socialization. As this home was centrally located and in an elevated area facing the village well, many people preferred to come. Also, we used to listen to the songs on the loudspeaker played the gramophone records.

The commotion of women and the Girka chappudu (noise of the pulley wheel) used for drawing water from wells starts early in the morning and in the evenings. People preferred to consume the clean, fresh water every day. So they never drank the stored water for many days. Once a woman fell in the well while drawing water, my brother-in-law saw and jumped in the well to save her.

The loud noise of cicadas in the summer was continuous mostly during the heat of the day. Close to them, the sound is more than 100 decibels. It is the mating call of the male cicadas. The sounds are made to attract the partners and for territoriality. The sound is not produced by vocal chords, but rather by the buckling of the ribs, the vibration of a membrane and amplification in the cavities of the cicada's abdomen.

The local variety of Mangoes was plenty. Some women were

bringing mangoes, Nalla jeedi pandlu and other local fruits in the baskets. In exchange of grains, they used to give them. From the Peddavagu people caught some fishes and sold in the village.

In the villages, the swings were tied to the Doolam (the wooden roof frame). Or sometimes climbed onto the Thottela (bed swing used for small babies) and enjoyed the swing.

Then slept in the afternoon for some time, as the summer heat sucks the energy and makes one drowsy after a heavy lunch. Late afternoon, played the Oman guntala peeta with dried tamarind seeds, or Ashta chemma and Paila pachisu with shells as dice and pawns. Girls and boys, young and old would play these games. I also went to play marbles with some children underneath a Neem tree.

Learn to swim

There were a few open farm wells near our home in Ramantha-pur. The farmlands are being converted into real estate and sold as plots for constructing buildings. The open wells remained abandoned for some years, and the local residents filled them with the garbage. I wanted to learn swimming, so it happened that I went with friends from our basti to one such abandoned wells which still had fresh water. Recently the farmer has sold all his land as plots, and this well is no more used for irrigation. This place was close to the Musi river, so there was plenty of water even in the middle of the summer. Then I was studying in seventh class. Senior friends suggested me to bring a five litres' gas nune dabba' i.e., the reuse tin can of Castrol oil. That was to help me to float. I took a small rope with me to tie it to my waist. I went along with the other gang of children from our Basti. There were many children swimming and jumping in the water. With a rope, I tied the tin can to my waist with the help of friends. Slowly went into the water by climbing down the steps in the well. Along the wall of the well, I started swimming. After a few rounds, as I was going into the deeper water suddenly found that the rope knot loosened and the tin can is floating above and I am sinking in the water! As all the children were busy swimming, I could not alert too. I got hold of the granite rocks by pushing my hand into the open gap of the well's wall. Slowly moved along the wall back to the steps and climbed up.

In one summer, my brother-in-law (my mother's brother's son) came from the village and said he would take me to the village for helping me to learn swimming. I had only 10 days of vacation and it was a very hot summer. He took me to Mamidipally my mother's birthplace. There was an open well close to the village with lots of water. The well was lined with granite rocks and had steps all the way to the bottom of the well. The local soil is black cotton soil, need to protect the walls otherwise in no time the well would collapse.

I remembered my mother telling an incident that happened in one such well in the village. Once a person came to take bath in the well and was washing clothes while sitting on the steps in the well close to the water. Suddenly a dead body surfaced from the well and started floating. Having seen this happening unexpectedly, he feared so much that he ran away from the well leaving the clothes then and there. He had severe motions after that and was in shock for several days. This particular lady committed suicide by jumping into this well and people were searching for her since three days and nobody knew that she jumped to death in this particular well. Those committing suicide often left their chappals near the well. To retrieve the submerged bodies, people often used Reni Campa (a thorny berries plant) tied to a rope dropped into the water. The dress stuck into this bush, the bodies are taken out of the well. With so many incidents happened in the past, while going to the well, I had my fears. What if there is someone drowned and yet to be surfaced.

Summer is the best time to learn swimming. The water would be warm and shallow. I was taken to a well, at around 10 a.m.

in the morning, being summer it was already very hot and I was sweating heavily. The first day, my brother-in-law requested a young boy returning from the well after swimming, to give his float. This float is a piece of dry Shagamatta plant trunk. Shagamatta is an agave plant, from a mature plant, a trunk emerges from the centre of the plant about 20 to 30 feet in height. It is one of the lightest wood materials available locally. It absorbs water very slowly, so every day after swimming, it should be dried. So we would keep it on the hot tin roof for drying in the sun. It has a diameter of about 20 to 30 centimetres. A piece of this wood about 2.5 feet in length is tied with paggam thallu (a thin rope used for tying the bullocks to control them). It is a very strong rope made with Janumu (Jute). We could see old people, especially in the summer, making such ropes by rolling Janumu on their thighs. It is tied to the waist in such a way that the piece of this wood is on the backside of the waist. It was not so convenient and painful at the waist, as the float pulled the body up through this rope.

Some children are afraid of water. Along with me, my brother-in-law wanted to take one boy called Raju. But having come to know brother-in-law's plan to take him to teach swimming, this boy started running all over the village. With the help of five other children finally, we could catch him. We all left to the well with him. This well was favourite for children as it is close to the village and had clean water. Many boys were swimming and diving already. There was shouting, and water splashing sounds. It had beautiful granite slab steps all the way down. It is well lined with granite blocks too. I took off the shirt, and with my Chaddi, I was ready. My brother-in-law tied the float and took me down the well over the steps. He asked me to make cups with my palms and push water underneath my belly continuously and start hitting the water with my two legs alternatively. I started practising it and soon it was convenient. I went to the well to reach the place where the steel pipes were submerged into the water, for drawing water attached to a diesel engine. It was so crowded with many other children enjoying the cools waters in hot summer. Some children were playing games such as diving deep and getting the soil from the bottom or finding a coin thrown intentionally. Hiding underneath the steps and inside the water holding the breath (police and thief game). Or catching someone by chasing. Some were bullying other small children by drowning them in the water for some time and making them cry. It was a mess altogether. I had to wade through this kind of situation to learn. But with scorching mid-summer bright and hot day, and the cool water also gave us a chance to escape from the hot weather. Being in the water and swimming was a pleasure. We returned home in the afternoon after spending 2 to 3 hours in the well and continued for the next eight days. By the time we returned home hungry and tired. Had some Ambali (hot gruel made with the flour of Sorghum or Ragi), Jonna rotte (Sorghum roti) with pickle and dal. And very little rice. Also ate lots of onions to beat the heat.

Within eight days, I could learn to swim. On the last day as I need to leave the village early. My brother-in-law wanted me to practice more before I left. He took me to the well again by 6:00 a.m. It was slightly chilly outside. He asked me to jump from the top of the well directly into the well. I jumped, the water was warm, and we both did swim for some time and left back to the city. For teaching my sons swimming, we had few swimming pools in the city, unlike the sweet memories I had.

Banamathi - Women's pshycological suffering

"Banamathi' is a forgotten word nowadays. About 30 years back and before, it was a common term heard in parts of Telangana. When some women used to have Banamathi, frequently women get into a trance. Some women cry hysterically; some call names of the people who did Banamathi to them; some swinging vigorously with hickups etc. and make some strange noises and shake their body. People considered it as a witchcraft performed on the victim by someone else intentionally. Some people say the enemies engage Mantragallu (the people who know Mantra or Tantra and invite the witches to pervade on them). As a result, so some people suffer from Banamathi.

In some villages, it was more prevalent than the others. In the rich families, the Banamathi was very less. In the poor families, women suffered Banamathi more. Otherwise, women suffering from Banamathi had different family problems. I have observed that as the family started earning a good income, the Banamathi started disappearing from such families. Also in those days girls got married at an early age say 7 years onwards, most of the children were 12 years old by the time they got married. There was always work continuously at home as the joint families were large in size, a minimum of 20 people in each family and also they need to work in the fields. This was a burden on the women. The insecurity and weakness of women in a family could be the reason, in disguise the women through Banamathi could let their emotions out.

People in villages identify some people as Mantragallu. Sometimes, they break their front two teeth, and some of them were killed by the villagers too. I heard that once there was a good Mantragadu, he asked four people to hold the legs of the cot, the cot moved with the men up over the steps and went into a room in the first floor and touched a pillow. Inside the pillow, a plastic doll was found with kumkum, turmeric, lemon and bangles. He is said to be having the power to cure women with Banamathi. No men ever got Banamathi. With the improvement in communication and Television at present, there is no one suffering from Banamathi. Probably any such cases are treated by the psychiatrist.

I was asking one of the women recently, why Banamathi is not much prevalent now in the same village as it used to be 30 years back. Her answer was simple, the Mantragallu are not there to do Banamathi now. Say in her village of about 400 families at least 40 women had Banamathi in the past.

Traditional Medicine

My mother and younger sister had jaundice almost every alternate year. Apart from having allopathic medicine plus lots of glucose to drink and eat they also had the traditional Chettu mandhu (herbal medicine plants) and followed Pathyam. Pathyam includes restrictions on what to eat and how to cook the food. Pathyam food is generally with no vegetable oil. Preferably had Sorghum roti with red chilli powder with garlic paste. There are some others along with Chettu mandhu they also recommend to have, cow's milk, sugar cane juice, puffed rice and sometimes mutton Biryani too.

The cause of jaundice was because we were drinking the water from the open well and probably it was contaminated. I always went to Rakamcherla a place close to Ghanapuram about 60 km West of Hyderabad city. There was a person who was giving Chettu mandhu . Its source is still kept as a secret by the person giving such a medicine. Every week he gave dose which is lumps of green leaves made into a paste. I bought for my sister and mother whenever they had jaundice. They got cured by this method and stringent pathyam.

White Horse

Cultural and traditional aspects of toddy consumption are interesting. People say drinking toddy is like getting on a white horse and ride.

Drinking is considered wrong in some cultures and religious faiths. For someone like me coming from Telangana State in India, it is a cultural practice, especially in the rural areas. Traditionally the toddy (palm wine) was the primary source of 'drink'. It is a natural and pure drink extracted from trees. It is called 'kallu' in Telugu, which is white in colour, tasting sweet and sour. It is an alcoholic beverage created from the sap of various species of palm trees such as the Palmyra (Thati Kallu) and Date palms (Eetha Kallu).

There is a particular community called "Gouds or Goundla," engaged in toddy tapping, and the collectors are called "Kallu Geetha Karmikulu," or Toddy Tappers. They traditionally collect Kallu every day morning and evening and make it available to the villagers. People collect toddy by climbing the Palmyra and date palm trees. Palmyra is one of the tallest trees. They had been collecting toddy from some of the trees since generations. They know the exact taste of Toddy from each tree. Climbing trees is the most difficult task, which they have learned with practice. They always wear a 'Budda Gochi" or small lion cloth for convenience to climb. They tie a thick rope around their waist and the tree they are climbing. This rope has rubbers too for increasing the friction. By pushing the body away and lifting both the feet to a higher hold they climb and by doing the reverse, they climb down. A small ring of rope connects the two legs for the extra grip on the tree trunk. Climbing toddy tree is no less an athletic feat!

The toddy is always tapped from a place just below the crown of the tree. They climb the tree carrying a sharp blade made of iron and clay pots to collect the toddy. They make a "Geetha" or cut exposing the sap near the neck of the tree. The sap is directed into the empty pots, with small guides. The pots are tied to the tree. When the plants are in a farmer's field, a Goud would harvest the toddy on a regular basis, in return, the landowner gets some part of Toddy as share. Rest they would sell to others in the village. In the past Toddy was never sold for money, the farmers shared part of their produce after harvesting for the Toddy served to them throughout the year, as part of a traditional jajmani system. The bonding between the consumer and the service provider was lifelong and intergenerational with both parties respecting the rights and obligations.

Eetha Kallu is very sweet and less intoxicating. Whereas, Thati Kallu is stronger (sweet in the morning, sour to bitter-sour in the evening after fermentation in the sun) and is highly intoxicating. People enjoy Kallu right at the trees where it is brought down. They drink out of leaves by holding them to their mouth while the Toddy tapper pours the Kallu from the Kallu Muntha (Toddy pot) like saaki serving liquor in madhushala. There are different types of toddy (Kallu) according to the season. Especially the toddy tapped during the summer from the male Palmyra trees is called "Pothu Thati

Kallu". Toddy is considered to cool the body from heat so there is more consumption of Toddy, especially during the summers. Besides, the yield of kallu in summer is manifold than normal yield during the year.

People suffering from Jaundice also consume Toddy as part of traditional medical treatment. The villagers might have less drinking water but the Kallu is plenty in some villages. When just collected afresh from the tree, it is very sweet and nice. It ferments and turns into alcohol with time. The toddy collected and consumed within 12 hours is good and has the effect of alcohol on the people who drink.

These days adulterated "Kallu" is being sold which also leads to addiction. When people stop consuming such Toddy they go insane. It is also called "Mandhu Kallu", meaning chemical made kallu. This is because the demand is more, and there are very few Palmyra trees left to meet the requirement. That is also because now it is sold to consumers, unlike the non-monetary transactions as part of the jajmani system (Indian economic system in which lower castes performed various functions for upper castes and received grain in return) in the past.

Commercialisation and business of liquor brewing started long back with the government taking monopoly over liquor and introducing "Indian Made Foreign Liquor" by National and International companies adding to government coffers in the form of excise duty. From the villages, in the form of taxes, a government may not get any revenue from agriculture produce, but they get considerable revenue from liquor sold.

However, toddy tapping is still not banned or taken over by the government recognized companies. With demand and supply gaps, due to increased population and vanishing palm trees, the toddy served today in villages is just artificial and chemical based chloroform intoxicant. Many people dependent on the traditional Toddy Tappers lost their livelihoods. The government considers liquor of any kind is bad, and at the same time encourages its selling through licenses that provide a lot of revenue to the state government. Habit and addiction of the people is a source of revenue for the government. Sometimes it is calculated that the source of income to the government from the sale of the liquor in a village is more than the total subsidies and freebies that the government gives to the same villagers. In that case, why Milk is never stopped from going out of the village. The government could have levied a higher tax on the consumers for the benefit of the farmers so that at least some milk the farmers could have consumed.

In the past toddy was sold in earthen pots specially designed with a wide bottom and narrow neck. I have seen most, Toddy sold in the glass bottles (called Kallu seesalu), such as reused beer bottles. Ironically in the past, it was sold in the reused Glucose glass (saline) bottles too. Toddy also has sugar, when a villager says the old man requires glucose', it means toddy. Some old people with arthritis walk straight with confidence after downing a bottle of Toddy. Nowadays saline comes in disposable plastic packets. The nickname of Toddy and other beverages is "mandhu" which means medicine in Telugu. The doctor prescribes for one's health, and the other is self-prescribed by the people for their happiness. Too much consumption of anything would finally lead to consuming the real medicine prescribed by a doctor.

When relatives come home, they are served Toddy as an honour. I was ten years old when I first tasted the Toddy. It happened that my family visited our relatives in the village Pulmamidi. They brought Toddy for the adults. It was kept in a place which is used for storing the onions called "Ulligadda Mande". It is a hut-like structure created with the dry sticks of pigeon pea plant. It is very cold inside. My 'Alludu' (cousin (sister) son) and I were alone sitting in that place as all the others were busy. He has shown me these Toddy bottles stored there for cooling. It was around 4:00 p.m. He said its taste is like sugar water and good to drink. I tasted a little bit, and it tasted so good. Soon, I have completed drinking three bottles, that is about two litres. I started feeling drowsy and soon fell into deep sleep. I am not sure what happened next. In the midnight, I called and woke up my mother telling that I am hungry. My mom said that I was in a deep sleep after consuming the toddy. They brought me home in a bullock cart from the field. First time in life drank so much that I was knocked out.

Most of the old generation people had the habit of drinking toddy. Men drink more than women, and they do almost regularly. Children don't drink, and they are discouraged. Men visit the "Kallu Compound" a place where Toddy is sold and also interact with friends. Women mostly sell the eateries. No person ever misbehaved with the women selling the eateries in such a place. They had lots of respect for them too. They sell items which are not found elsewhere, such as very big size Papadalu, Ulavalu (Horse gram), Bobbarlu (cowpeas), Chenagalu (Chick Pea), Chudva (Puffed rice plus other ingredients), Mirchi bajji, boiled eggs, etc. These items being slightly spicy were always tasty. I always loved to eat those items.

Drinking is common for nearly all kinds of occasions or events. Birth and death of a person is also an occasion to drink. Happiness is an obvious reason to celebrate. And anything sad is more a reason to drink. Many habituated people, of course, drink every day for no reason too. On the day of death of a person, people cry so much in sadness. To forget the sorrow, some of the relatives offer Toddy to the bereaved family members. It is called 'Chedu Idavali' or lose the bitterness. During happy occasions, the host provides the Toddy, and during the sad occasions, the guests sponsor the toddy to the family members.

The agriculture labour called for work in one's field is often given day's wage and also a bottle of toddy. This is a common practice for both men and women labourers. In some places, the men have two bottles. Struggles for wage hike succeeded in some areas. Agriculture coolies would render the service because the landlords ensure the agreed toddy bottles. They say only by drinking they could get deep sleep and forget the pains of a day's hard work and be prepared for the next day's work. I met an old couple involved in pottery in Peddamaduru village they cook their evening meal by 4:30 p.m. and consume the fresh Toddy and sleep before 7 p.m. They woke up early morning by 5:00 a.m. This routine was good for their health and lived happily and making pottery even in their 80s.

In the rural villages, both women and men work equally. Sometimes women work more than men. Toddy is a family drink in our families, especially among the older generation. Except for children and few adults, everyone drinks Toddy. In quantity, women won't drink much and as regularly compared to men. Sometimes a son drinks and takes Toddy to the aged parents. It is a kind of respect and honour.

After drinks, I saw women speak on par with men. They talk with an open heart even with their husbands, and there is no hatred in their minds. The jovial mood of the whole family makes a day complete with some toddy. In villages, every occasion is cherished with drinks and made memorable. Why ignore or deny a cool farewell to the day, after all so much unpleasant order of daily life despite complaints, curses and struggles don't change immediately.

Of late beer and whiskey is replacing toddy. It is a burden on the people and also not so good for the health of the people consuming. It benefits only the multi-billion liquor barons and never addresses the social and local environmental issues.

There is a festival called "Bonalu" celebrated in reverence to the Goddess Durga. There are many names to Goddess Durga geographically like Yellamma, Maisamma, etc. Sacrificing the animals and offering toddy is common in many temples. They pour toddy before the entrance gate of the temple, called "Saka Pettadam". It is an offering to the deity. They also let the sacrificial animal drink some quantity of toddy before sacrificing it in front of the temple. Probably they don't want the slaughtered animal suffer extremely at the time of death.

The culture of tribals

Once EFICOR (NGO) asked me to evaluate the project they have implemented, i.e., 'Food security and Livelihoods project,'. The stakeholders were the vulnerable Malto tribal community living in Rajmahal area near the foothills of the Himalayas, Jharkhand State. I was very much interested in this evaluation. Malto people are very cultured, consider the guest as the most important person and give the highest respect. When I walked with the EFICOR team to one of the villages, they were ready with flowers and water. I learnt that they wanted to wash my feet with water on a big plate. I politely declined their request. Their simplicity touches me. Tribals are living in the remote areas in the forests.

Once in a village near Kuntala waterfalls, Adilabad district, Telangana State, I went to the house of a tribal head. There were so many chickens around; I asked why so many? He said that they are mostly for the guests or visitors, including the government officers who occasionally visit their village. Their simplicity, honesty and respect for guests could be another reason for their exploitation historically by the so-called civilised people living in villages and towns.

In the villages around Jagdalpur, Chhattisgarh State, the local tribals greeted us with flowers and a garland. Almost in every tribal culture that I have visited I observed great respect for guests as a distinct element of their culture. Also, I found them worshipping animate and inanimate objects in Nature. Agricultural practices are predominantly need-based coupled with several customs and traditions of conservation. They have festivals to thank Nature, before consuming fruits, vegetables and crops. Nature's kindness is acknowledged by them through their customs and practices. Sharing the resources with kins and villagers and joint cultivation is still a common practice. Role of money is minimal in their economy. One could see them using the money, whatever little they, in weekly shandy for buying products that come from outside. The tribals also respect petty traders, GCC employers, small contractors and government employees. Unfortunately, the outsiders have been displacing the tribals from their land and forest. Much of the conflicts in tribal areas would be resolved if the so-called civilised people from outside learnt to respect the host.

Poor and destitute

People often discuss poverty and poor. Unless one was poor and experienced poverty, it is not possible to understand what is poverty or to be poor. One may partly succeed to realize by being sensitive and keenly observing the poor and listening to the narratives and concerns of the marginalised and poor. In one of the projects, we wanted to support the poorest of the poor. Therefore, to understand, I started searching for the poorest of the poor in the villages. Wanted to know who are they? And how are they? In a village, during the focused group discussion with the community, it is easy to get the list of very poor families. Usually, they don't attend meetings or village gatherings. They also live in isolation or away from the main community. I still remember having seen one old very poor lady in a village about 18 years back, in Mahabubnagar district, Telangana state. She was the most miserable person in the village among the poor and also destitute. When she came out of her makeshift hut, I saw her frail body holding a stick in her hand, and all her hair was white. She lives on the food given by others through compassion. She could not speak much and also did not ask anything from me. Her picture still lingers in my mind whenever I think of the poor.

During an evaluation, I wanted to understand the food security of the Malto tribals. Visited some of the households to see the grains that they have stored in their home and how long they would last for consumption? What do they eat every day? Do they have kitchen gardens and domestic livestock to supplement their food needs? How the natural resources are existing, which would support their livelihoods? Do they have alternative livelihood opportunities? etc. I found that they store grains to last for months, as their production or income is seasonal and also at risk. With limited access to the Minor Forest Produce, or non-timber forest produce as it is also called, from the forests, the food security and dependence of the tribals is at risk. The carrying capacity of their immediate environment is also reduced.

Poverty doesn't defeat pride

Once in Bundelkhand, I was doing an impact assessment of a project. It was late evening. There was no power in the village. There was one solar street light where I was discussing with the villagers. I saw one girl sitting at a distance studying under the solar street light. I was inspired by her passion for learning. She was poor inhabiting a remote village, but her willingness to know learn in spite of the challenges inspired me.

I had been visiting Azadpur, a village in the remote Mau Block in Chitrakoot, Uttar Pradesh State. I visited the village in 2012, 2014 and 2017. This particular habitation was selected by EFICOR for a project, as it falls under the Bundelkhand drought-prone region. It is a rocky area with very thin soil. They belong to scheduled caste and very poor.

In 2012 when I visited the streets were dusty, and the houses did not look clean. Majority of the homes had no plaster. I saw amazing children there, I took their pictures. I liked two girls who were very young, and their smile attracted me. They were playing at that time. One of the girls had ear-rings out of neem leaf spines. The other girl was wearing a thread attached with Iron ring. I liked this picture especially for the smile and language of their eyes. I also took pictures of two other girls; they too looked so sharp. There was pride in everyone in spite of whatever they are. I revisited the same habitation in 2014 and 2017. Went to the same place and enquired about the children by showing them their earlier photographs. Retook their pictures. I could not meet some children as they were not present at that time. In every picture, year by year, I could see how their habitation transformed and also the change in their looks. Delighted to observe something constant - their pride has not come down in any way. Pride is through accepting and accomplishing all the challenges in life with dignity. These people have seen and experienced all the shades in their life. They had an unprecedented wealth; nobody can rob.

Sacrificing villages for development

The life and livelihood of the farmers living in Nakka vagu basin are affected beyond repair and compensation due to so-called development through industrialisation.

After choosing the area for my Doctorate, I have visited the place for the first time in the year 1995. I still remember the strong unpleasant smell that greets one the moment one gets down the bus at Patancheru which is about 2 km from the Nakka Vagu (which means Fox stream in Telugu). Mr Prashanth, my friend, accompanied me to the field area. As we moved to some of the villages, we saw brick kilns in once fertile lands. The contractors have engaged the poor people from Orissa State to work for brick making, where the children were also working. There are very few standing crops, and they were not healthy. There are two streams with polluted water flowing in the area: Nakka Vagu (Fox Stream) and Pamula Vagu (Snakes Stream). We saw that some sheep were drinking the coloured and obnoxious water from the Pamula Vagu, and shepherds washing their hands and feet in the same waters. I was touched by the plight of the people in the region. We heard stories that in some of the pools of water in the area, when a buffalo went for a bath, its skin peeled off because the water was so acidic, its pH was less than four.

Prof. K. Purushotham Reddy and Dr Kishan Rao were

fighting for the rights of the people since more than a decade already in the area. They have recorded the blue baby syndrome or a baby born due to excess pollutants entering into the conceived mother. The skin rashes are easy to be found. From cancer to all kinds of impacts on the internal and external bodies of the people were also observed upon investigation by doctors. Women had often abortions too. Rice cultivated using the polluted water, smelled, turned yellow and spoiled by evening.

Saw an ancient sculpture, the local Hindus have applied a vermillion to it. It is probably a sculpture of more than 1000 years old, was representing either Buddhism or Jainism. Upon enquiry, someone said it was found while excavating the soil for brick making and was kept on the roadside. They said many such statues were found in the area. In business who cares about the history and the relics. I went to the Archaeology department and learnt there is a continuous history of people living in the area since the 2nd Century BC. It means the land which sustained agriculture since then has become infertile and unsustainable due to the so-called industrial development.

Pollution of water, soil and air may be the main cause of fallow lands. On the whole, about 20% of the farms were left fallow in most of the villages. Traditionally there had been two types of irrigation practices in the region, lift irrigation from wells and streams, and irrigation by gravity from tanks. The lifts worked with bullocks called mhota are suitable for irrigating up to 8 acres. Mhotas were in practice till the 1980's. The present practice of lift irrigation is by electric motor pumps. The availability of water from some tanks spread in the region can also be attributed to the prosperity of agriculture. Tanks are adequate in numbers, but now many such tanks are of little use except as storage ponds for industrial effluents. As these tanks are connected in series, the pollutants entering a tank at higher reaches pollutes all other tanks downstream. Presently many farmers shifted to dry-land farming as the water sources are polluted. The pollution of wells and tanks crippled all those farmers irrigating crops under them.

People don't have access to the drinking water in the area. Some of the villagers were buying water or they were paying for the water supplied by the Government and sometimes buying from private agencies. By the end of my PhD, I have filed a Public Interest Litigation in the High Court of Andhra Pradesh to provide free drinking water under the polluter pays principle. The order came immediately, and the villagers are being provided free drinking water. Sad, the court had to intervene to ensure drinking water which they had from any of the sources since centuries in the region.

A village failed to offer a cup of tea

Mr Dharamraj Ranka had many Goshalas in Hyderabad. Of the three major abattoirs existing in India at that time, two were in Telangana. The cattle sold in the region were slaughtered and the beef was locally consumed or exported to the middle east. As a result, the cattle numbers in the state reduced. The small and marginal farmers dependent on the cattle for farming were suffering. Therefore a study was proposed by Mr Dharamraj Ranka under the leadership of Prof. K. Purushotham Reddy. Including myself, a team of 6 people visited several villages, cattle markets and interviewed people to assess the situation. The team travelled parts of Telangana extensively. I have taken photographs of the illegal transportation of the cattle at great risk. The brokers did not allow us to do the study. Once we went to a village called Chautkur near Jogipet, Medak district, Telangana and requested for a cup of tea. They could not get a glass of milk in the whole village. Due to declining cattle, commercialization of milk production and selling milk to urban areas, they could not provide a cup of tea. We made a statement "Chautkur pote chai dorkaledu" i.e., Couldn't get a cup of tea in Chautkur village. This is the fate of villages where farmers consume less and sell almost everything. Based on the information collected, a report was prepared titled "Game of Numbers" - with details on the situation of cattle. A public interest litigation was filed in the supreme court of India with all the data to stop the abattoirs and illegal slaughtering of the cattle. That was also critical to address the needs of the small and marginal farmers. We got an interim order from the supreme court based on the report and findings.

Traditional green buildings

I got into the basics of understanding the traditional houses that I had seen in the villages, and I still love them.

In the villages, during my visits and stay, I observed the use of local materials for construction; necessary spaces were created for use; easy for maintenance; they had cultural and aesthetic values; living spaces meet the aspirations of people; spaces created which could bring peace and enhance one's spirituality. The natural interacting aspects, such as light, air circulation, the flow of water; temperature and relative humidity were also considered. Being an environmentalist, everything was understood. Based on the above observations, I was giving lectures. Sometimes the architecture students and builders said that what I taught was practical and not found in their textbooks.

While developing the GEO Research centre, I was conscious to build the environment-friendly structures mostly using local materials, and reuse of materials. The thumb rule was that they should be maintenance free and low-cost. Constructed one room with Pati-Matti as in villages many houses were built in the past. Pati Matti is the old soil or earth, procured from the place where once a village existed. It is the remnant soil of a degraded or disintegrated village which existed in the past. It had all the pieces of evidence of the people living there such as pottery shards, pieces of charcoal, bones, broken bangles, slag, shells, etc. This soil is resistant to erosion and had outstanding compactness and strength.

The challenge was to identify the person to construct the house. About 30 years back the last house was built with mud walls. I found one old person in the village who had some experience of constructing the mud-walls during his youth. I requested him to guide the young labour in preparation of the material and support in the construction of the house with mud. To get the Pati-Matti, I searched the fields near a 500 years old temple around which the village existed in the past. Now it is a field. I found all the pieces of evidence of the village in the soil. I requested the farmer to give me the soil from his field. He agreed, and I collected the soil and brought it to the Geo-Research Center.

The construction of the mud-walls happens in phases. One cannot construct as much as one wants in a day as it is done with the bricks. Only 2 to 3 feet height wall can be constructed in a day. Then it should dry completely for adding another layer of few more feet wall over it. To reach a height of 15 feet, it took more than a one-month time.

First, the pati-matti is soaked in water and pressed with legs to create a good clay. The balls of clay are prepared and passed on to the person sitting and constructing the wall. The mud ball is pressed to form layers of the wall. Even the smoothening is done by bare hands and fingers. The streets in the villages are designed to be narrow, to prevent the erosion of walls from rain, wind, diurnal temperature variation. As this structure was in the centre, I need to protect it from the walls, therefore with a chicken mesh wire as a layer made rough plastering with the cement. Plastering was done inside the room with dubba matti (a fine soil). The sil koyya (sticks for hanging) things, a shelf with doors and two windows were made in the traditional way. The two-winged door is also traditional.

I love the earthen structures because it is like living in the Mother Earth lap. They cause less impact on the environment as the embodied energy is very low. It is always locally available and accessible. Even a poor person, can build a house like a bird builds a nest when it is needed. One could start construction of house without big plans of procuring or importing the exotic materials from elsewhere. Very fewer tools are used. The bare hands and legs are mostly used for preparing the material. There is no need to depend on outside experts for the construction.

I observed how the tribals construct and maintain their houses with great love. As they are constructed by themselves, the houses reflect their aspirations, needs and aesthetics. They have great love and pride in living the space they made into a home. With maintenance, they always looked new and with the floral and animals designs/drawings on the walls which bring their life world to live with them. They know that space belongs to all and they are only occupying for sometime in space and time. Everything should disintegrate and one day would be part of the same soil where one would rest after death.

Wild animals love some villages

There was a drastic difference between the villages where the Bishnoi community lived and the villages with Non-Bishnoi people. The animal's density was very high, and they roamed close to the Bishnoi villages. There is a historical reason why the wild animals loved to stay close to Bishnoi community habitations.

During the visit to Bishnoi community villages in Haryana for a study, Mr Vinod narrated the story of a lady named Amrita Devi. She is a member of the sect who inspired as many as 362 other Bishnois to go to their deaths in protest of the cutting down of Khejri trees in September 1730. The Khejri tree that is Prosopis cineraria is also considered to be sacred by the Bishnois. The Maharajah of Jodhpur, Abhay Singh, requiring wood for the construction of a new palace, sent soldiers to cut trees in the village of Khejarli, which was called Jehnad at that time. Noticing their actions, Devi hugged a tree in an attempt to stop them. Her family then adopted the same strategy, as did other local people when the news spread. She told the soldiers that she considered their actions to be an insult to her faith and that she was prepared to die to save the trees. The soldiers did indeed kill her and others until Abhay Singh was informed of what was going on and intervened to stop the massacre. This is the commitment of the Bishnoi community. And I was there to address one of their problems.

With Mr Vinod, I started in a vehicle to see the wildlife in the area. Badopal is a village, about 10km away from Fatehabad town. In the areas around this village, there are 500 nos of Blackbucks, Neelgai (blue bull), deer, and other wildlife inhabit the area. The Government of India planned a Nuclear Power Plant at the Village Gorakhpur and acquired land for the plant, housing and other utilities. They made a fence of steel wire all around the acquired places. The place acquired for the township had Blackbucks, Neelgai (Blue Bull), Deer and other wildlife. They had restrictions on their movement, and some of the animals have stuck in the barbed fence have died recently. During the visit, I could see herds of animals roaming freely in the area.

More smoke-less fire

One day I was in a village trying to understand the rural energy situation. I observed that there was heaps of fuelwood stored in the courtyards of many houses. This fuelwood was collected, for use in cooking for several months. It was harvested from the village commons and the nearby-degraded scrubland. I found that, on an average, people spend up to four days in a month collecting fuelwood. Considering the rural wage rates being currently offered under government programs, it amounts to no less than Ten USD a month. Where most of the rural poor earn around only one USD per day. Their spending on fuelwood sometimes works out costlier than the Liquid Petroleum Gas (LPG) supplied by the government through a range of subsidies.

Randomly I visited about 50 household kitchens which changed my life. I noticed that about half of the stoves were of 'three-stone' stove type and the rest made from clay. Such stoves were highly inefficient, rudimentary and primitive. I will never forget those visits; they made me realise how a large number of people are still stuck with them and exposed to their harmful effects.

The stoves and the kitchens do not reflect the changes in the lives of the families over the generations. Many people are now living in concrete houses, eating high-value food, can afford mobile phones, and send their children to English-medium private schools, but they don't have a good and efficient stove. Despite all the winds of change and development, the kitchen remains a smoky place with dark-soot walls and the roof. Even traditionally, kitchens have occupied relatively small spaces inside or outside the house.

I myself declared that my first step would be creating awareness about indoor air pollution and its harmful effects. I went to communities and showed them pictures of their stoves through a projector. Although people-in-general were interested in watching the slideshow, women objected when it came to seeing their own stoves. This is because the kitchen was not a place of pride for them, even though they respect the stove very much. I then explained to the communities the impact of indoor air pollution and its multiplier effects on them. They were quite interested in adopting efficient stoves, but they were helpless, as they did not have access to them.

In one of the villages, the state government promoted chimney stoves with grates this is about 15 years back. Those stoves were nowhere to be found. Within a few years, the stoves had disintegrated, the chimneys were choked with soot, the grates were burnt down, and the stoves disappeared. The design of the stoves did not take into account how adaptable they were to local conditions and practices. The stoves were distributed under a government scheme and were also highly subsidised. The stoves were not accepted, and therefore the sustainable demand from the local community did not exist.

This exposure made me sensitive towards the issue of stoves in the rural areas, and I was motivated to help and improve their stoves' design. I realised that there could not be a single globally accepted good stove design to meet the local needs. As the challenge was adapting designs to meet the local needs.

As I started off, I could not easily access specialists in the field of good stoves. However, through the internet, I found numerous, and diverse stove designs that evolved around the globe – in response to a variety of food habits, cooking methods, cultural traditions, types of available biomass for fuel, family size, etc. Studying them formed the basis of my initial understanding of stoves, and I continued the research and designed the stoves to meet the specific community needs. In a span of 5 years, I designed more than 50 biomass stoves, which were low-cost efficient and adoptable by the communities as per their requirement for diverse geographies and food habits of the people. Facilitated the stoves in parts of India and abroad. All the information on stove designs was written as a book titled "Understanding Stoves", MetaMeta, Netherlands published it. All my work on stoves was declared as open knowledge or creative commons for the common good.

A stove is not just a stove or a piece of equipment, it has so many values around which are addressed by its use. Reducing the drudgery of women in cooking and in accessing the fuelwood. The health of the women and children is improved through less-emissions. Time is saved for women to spend on other aspects required to improve quality of life. The local biomass and biodiversity are conserved. Mitigating smog and CO2 emissions which is a cause of global warming and climate change. There are so many values around this simple initiative widely, and I feel very fortunate and happy, for working on this aspect and popularized it widely.

Sustainable Rural Livelihoods

I am fortunate for having had several opportunities in my life to have vast experience of working with the rural communities. That involved travelling across India including some of the remote areas. Directly or indirectly my work was related to the sustainability of rural livelihoods.

This work required an understanding of how people in villages are connected to the natural resources and making a living. The resources sustainability is critical for their existence and also for addressing the food security and other basic needs of people. The urban areas are existing and thriving at the cost of degradation of the rural regions and environment.

Sustainable rural livelihoods are one of the most significant challenges of the 21st Century. The Sustainable Development Goals has prime relevance to the rural development issues in developing countries. A multi-pronged approach is needed for achieving sustainability of the rural areas.

Several rural development programs are being implemented through funding from Government, Non-government, National and International agencies. There is a paradigm shift in rural development approaches, i.e., adaptive rural livelihoods strategies are evolved and are being practiced.

There is a progressive change brought in the watershed projects being implemented in the semi-arid and arid areas.

Earlier water used to be the single major output[h2] around which livelihoods were perceived. Now the latest thinking evolved is "Watersheds is an Approach and Livelihoods a Programme". It is proved that during the drought and especially in the context of climate change, the Natural Resources related livelihoods are not sustainable and often could not prevent migrations. And also in the post-watershed project scenario the livelihood options and opportunities of poor people, resource-poor people and women were at stake.

The adaptive Livelihood strategies include a) Diversification – Each family and individual needs to be capable to adopt more than one livelihood; b) Adopting the secondary and tertiary sector livelihoods i.e., Non Natural Resource related livelihoods are also given priority, and There should be programs with focus on empowerment of Poor and Women.

Insecure rural livelihoods cannot ensure protection and rejuvenation of environment and natural capital. Promotion of sustainable rural livelihoods has to invariably ensure a better quality of resource structure of the community and region. Budget allocations and piecemeal interventions are no substitute for eco-friendly sustainable rural livelihoods strategy.

Smart villages

Since the beginning of my professional life, I was closely associated with community development interventions. People in the villages work very hard compared to the urban areas. Hard work empowers and leads communities towards sustainable development. Access and use of technologies in the respective work make one smart. Several technologies developed in recent times are adopted by the rural communities across India.

I was interested in studying how 'Smart Villages' would enable the communities and individuals to take smart decisions collectively using smart technologies, communication, and innovations.

To increase the irrigation potential, the solar-powered motor pumps for the borewells were also suggested. The remote and most deserving poorer communities could access the off-grid solar power and improve their livelihoods.

The farmers could adopt the low-cost soil moisture sensors in their fields. The sensors installed at various depths would make the farmers understand the fluctuations in moisture levels. The farmers would manage drainage and irrigation based on the information received from the sensors. Enabled by GSM the data could be received on the mobile phones too.

Understanding the spatial resources helps in efficient decision making. In this context apart from the imageries such as google maps, and drones could be used with higher resolution for monitoring and management of resources. Drones fitted with cameras enable one to access spatial and temporal information for management of crops and water use efficiency. The local school children and teachers could be trained in flying the drones for identification of the areas affected by various pests. The farmers could plan the harvesting and other management practices based on the observations made from the images obtained from the drone. Solar powered 360 degrees cameras fitted to the Balloon kites (Kytoon / Helikite), and zooming are ideal for continuous monitoring of the resources. At least 4 or 5 such ballon kites could be deployed in a village to cover an extent about 500 to 1000 acres.

Automatic Weather Stations enabled with Wi-Fi, give continuous information on the weather. The farmers by understanding, especially the temperature and relative humidity could manage their crops better. With the availability of the local weather data, they could go for the index based insurance from the Government and other agencies. Also, they could better manage their crops and do irrigation scheduling.

Smart application for the mobile phones developed would enable farmers to register their category of produce, quantity and their expected price and get the right price for their produce. The farmers can know agriculture commodities rates live through web streaming of agriculture markets or from agriculture market information network.

The villager could interact with line department officials through video conferencing facilities at the community centres. They could also access the e-services for utility.

The local health workers could facilitate the telemedicine services to the deserving people, especially women, children and old people.

With mobile smartphones currently used by most of the people, there are many possibilities for smart monitoring and management. The villages are no more traditional villages with improved communication and access to information. The smart and hard-working farmers have a better chance to reduce vulnerabilities in the present scenario.

I was instrumental in establishing two village knowledge centres for the MS Swaminathan Foundation during the implementation of the projects at Srirangapur village in Mahabubnagar district, Balaji Thanda near Miryalaguda town in Telangana State and Kondrapole village near Narsaraopeta town in Andhra Pradesh. A village knowledge centre has the necessary infrastructure (computers, printers, webcam, public address system, etc.), knowledge and services. There are myriad other ways possible to turn our villages into Smart Rural India.

Digital education to the farmers and other professional communities in the villages is necessary. Learning is a continuous process. The digital content developed by the best teachers in the local language and dialect facilitates many to learn and get updated with the technologies and practices. With access to increased internet bandwidth, the content is cheaper and easily accessible.

Farmers

By occupation farmer is the one who is connected with earth more than anyone else. Why a farmer is not honored, he is becoming more and more vulnerable? Over a period, this sector turned from sustainable agriculture to exploitative agriculture. The new practices are degrading the very resources which sustained farming. The soil degradation, water pollution, groundwater depletion, pesticide residues in the produce, greenhouse gasses release, etc., are some of the impacts. The scientific community and the policy makers introducing GMOs, chemical-based agriculture, etc., are also responsible for this pathetic situation.

If the budget component allocated to the farmers and agriculture sector increases every year means, we have not achieved much. If the annual budget allocation to the farm sector decreases, it means we are actually working and developing this sector. It is like the number of pills taken by a patient continues or increases, it does not mean that the patient is becoming healthy.

In the history, the farmers paid the taxes and contributed to the economy of the nations. Earliest civilizations and cultures in parts of the world flourished. The richest kings, kingdoms, monuments existed because of farmers' contributions. Today our policies, technologies, and other factors made the farmer no less than a beggar for everything - seeds, fertilizers, support prices, loans, insurance, power, rains (cloud seeding), water for irrigation, etc. There is a need for serious thought and strategy for the sustainability of farming and farmers' livelihood.

We love farmers and their well-being because they provide food, fodder, fibre, fuel and much more. Why we are not happy when the prices of their produce go up? There were jokes and anger when the price of onions increased. No one was bothered when the farmers had been at a loss many times, and even paying to dump the produce as garbage. I once dumped flowers as trash, cultivated on our Farm as the price was so low. In general, farmer rarely gets profits that he deserves for the efforts. Farmers feel sorry when the whole system conspires to bring down the prices when they rarely get a good price. On the whole, it is common sense to understand that the prices go high for various reasons such as a particular crop production was not high due to crop failure. In such a case, the farmer would get compensated through increase in price and so the dependent people.

First of all, every farmer deserves the right price for the produce. Paying the right price means we are not exploiting a farmer and also giving due respect to the farmer and the agriculture sector. A farmer lives happily with honour and dignity only when they could sell the produce at a right price with some profit, after deducting expenses on the inputs, labour, processing, etc.

The petrol and gold price also comes down, but not the water price. In the packaged water business, no one ever says how the price of a water bottle reduced. Even during the rainy season, the price of water is the same. There was never an offer like: one bottle free for every bottle purchase; 20% extra water for the same price; or free gifts on purchase of a water bottle. When water is an important input for agriculture, why the produce of the farmer should be undervalued. The state ensures the minimum wages for people working in all sectors, how come the state has never protected the minimum wages of farmers, by ensuring the minimum support to the farmers. Where are the labour inspectors in agriculture sector.

In the history, farmers were givers, i.e., taxpayers and contributed to the GDP of the nation. But they are now at the receiving end. Over the last 50 years, the pride of the farmers was belittled by the systems. Everyone around the farmer is getting benefited through exploitation but not the real farmer. The government officials, university professors, research scientists, and civil society representatives are happy with their profession. There are multinational companies benefited by selling seeds, pesticides, fertilizers, technologies, processing goods and selling the produce. The brokers and other middlemen are also becoming rich. The debt-ridden farmers are becoming poorer and few are also committing suicides. The dependent secondary stakeholders are not supporting the farmers. Whenever there is a sudden increase in prices, in the interest of destitute people, it is the discretion of the government to subsidize the goods.

In the past there was pride to say "I am a farmer," because farmers rarely depended on the government systems. Farmer was independent before India got independence, but after independence farmer has become dependent. Our system failed in promoting Gram Swaraj, otherwise the fate of farmers would not have been so bad. Farmers before independence were paying the tax to the then rulers. None of the rulers nor kingdoms ever had any debt in the past. At present, every nation is in debt, in billions of dollars. The debt is also on just born babies and those yet to be born. And we never know when this debt would be cleared. The civilizations, culture, and traditions flourished with the development, progress of agriculture, and surplus food production. The great monuments stand testimony to the prosperous agriculture-based economy in the past.

In the past, the development systems based on the primary sector such as agriculture was more sustainable. All the communities existed as a social network and promoted farming. The farmers had pride. Since last two decades, the farmers' contribution to the economic development of the nation is least considered, although majority of the population is still dependent on the agriculture sector. This is because of undervaluing the price of produce and labour. With the green revolution, the farmer's dependency on the non-sustainable input systems increased. The increased production is at the cost of degraded environment and ecological systems. The ecological footprint of the farmer is growing. The contribution of the greenhouse gasses emissions from the agriculture sector is also increasing. The vulnerability of agriculture sector is growing from newer dimensions such as climate change, pollution, environmental degradation, GM crops, etc.

Today, the economy is becoming more and more virtual, which is based on printed money, petrodollars, shares, and inflation. The farmers are contributing to the real economy through production. Through right price to the farmer, we could restore the pride of their farmer and also address the food security of the nation. Then the farmers hand would be a 'giving hand' rather a 'receiving hand.' The farmers would give up all the subsidies, get paid worth their labour, would employ people, adopt technologies, pay for power and water, etc. They would be no more at the mercy of policies. The farmer would also pay taxes for the development of the resources and social security. Once again we would see debt-free nations.

We are not sensitive to farmers; they are taken for granted. The day will come when everyone realizes the basis of our own existence.

About the Author

Dr Sai Bhaskar Reddy Nakka is a multifaceted person with varied interests. Travelled extensively in parts of India and many other countries. Based on his intricate observations and understanding tries to bring change and development. Contributed in the areas of rural development, sustainability, environment, climate change, energy, agriculture and water. Has more than 100 innovations and designs declared them as open knowledge.

You can connect with me on:
🌐 http://saibhaskar.com

www.ingramcontent.com/pod-product-compliance
Lightning Source LLC
Chambersburg PA
CBHW051356250726
48656CB00006B/2119